Flooded Canyon

Ross Gibson

Ross Gibson is Centenary Professor of Creative & Cultural Research at the University of Canberra. He works collaboratively on books, films, artworks and strategic-planning exercises, and he supervises postgraduate students in similar pursuits. His main interests lie in contemporary arts, communication and the history of environmental consciousness in colonial cultures, particularly in Australia and the Pacific.

During the early 2000s he was Creative Director for the establishment of the Australian Centre for the Moving Image at Federation Square in Melbourne. Prior to that, while working at the University of Technology in Sydney, he was a Senior Consultant Producer during the development and inaugural years of the Museum of Sydney. Over the past two decades he has also held Professorial posts at UTS and the University of Sydney.

Recent works include the books *Changescapes* (2015), *Memoryscapes* (2015), *The Criminal Re-Register* (2017), *reDACT* (2019), plus the ABC Radio National feature *Green Love* (2016), and the public artwork Bluster Town, commissioned for Wynyard railway station by Transport NSW. His serialised photographic poem, Accident Music, was published online weekly with the Justice & Police Museum in Sydney (2010–2013).

A fellow of the Australian Academy of Humanities, he has served on the Boards of Directors for several public agencies and has been a member of the foresighting team for the Prime Minister's Science, Engineering and Innovation Council.

Books by Ross Gibson

The Diminishing Paradise: Changing Literary Perceptions of Australia, 1984.

Toward New Holland, ed. Ross Gibson, 1986.

South Pacific, ed. Ross Gibson, 1988.

South of the West: Postcolonialism and the Narrative Construction of Australia, 1992.

The Bond Store Tales, 1996.

Exchanges: Cross-cultural Encounters in Australia and the Pacific, ed. Ross Gibson, 1996.

Seven Versions of an Australian Badland, 2002.

Remembrance + The Moving Image, ed. Ross Gibson, 2003.

Interaction: Systems, Practice and Theory, eds. Ernest Edmonds and Ross Gibson, 2004.

New Beginnings; classic paintings from the Corrigan Collection of 21st Century Aboriginal art, Emily McCulloch with Ross Gibson, 2008.

The Summer Exercises, 2008.

VO1CE: vocal aesthetics in digital arts and media, eds. Norie Neumark, Ross Gibson and Theo van Leeuwen, 2010.

26 Views of the Starburst World: William Dawes at Sydney Cove 1788–1791, 2012.

By-Roads and Hidden Treasures: mapping cultural assets in regional Australia, eds. Paul Ashton, Chris Gibson and Ross Gibson, 2015.

Stone Grown Cold (poetry), 2015.

Changescapes: complexity, mutability, aesthetics, 2015.

Memoryscopes: remnants, forensics, aesthetics, 2015.

The Criminal Re-Register (poetry), 2017.

Basalt, 2017.

reDACT (poetry), 2019.

Ross Gibson

Flooded Canyon

UPSWELL

First published in Australia in 2023
by Upswell Publishing
Perth, Western Australia
upswellpublishing.com

ISBN: 978-0-645-53687-4

A catalogue record for this book is available from the National Library of Australia

Cover design by Chil3, Fremantle
Typeset in Foundry Origin by Lasertype

Upswell Publishing is assisted by the State of Western Australia through its funding program for arts and culture.

Department of
Local Government, Sport and Cultural Industries
GOVERNMENT OF
WESTERN AUSTRALIA

Love and thanks, always, Kathryn Bird.

*And special thanks to Peter Emmett,
for the title, and for much else.*

This is what the drone-cam sees:

> the vast rift in Sydney's sandstone canyon
> has been
> flooded
> up and down
> and all across
> so that time keeps aching
> stopless,
> tidal,
> ever-pressed,
> to show,
> in time,
> a full and fourth dimension in a fabled Harbour.

Next hear this:

> at sea-level, within the city-scape,
> recorded birdsong loops incessant
> in a concrete-cancered music bowl

> while

> essential city services
> are outsourced *ex officio*
> to a Tuvaluan ponzi scheme

and

 bitcoins sea-change back to petro-bucks
 inside
 some brand new Harbour-bottom ruse.

Which brings these visions into view:

 the animated flip-book of an actual town
 that is
 akimbo-skewed and synchronised to show
 Kenneth Slessor's flooding time,
 the time that does not flow

plus

there's an electric storm now roiling endless,
stark and coruscating
behind your eyelids when they blink

such that

a blur hangs always floating
at the overlap

of what is but also seems.

Then

    a kayak gyres arse-up
    in the vortexed waterwakes
    of two Manly Ferries
    backing up

while

    a candy-coloured hazmat van,

purrs air-conditioned in a cul-de-sac

and

clumps of verdure pinched from elsewhere
distend over-ripe and extra-moist
inside a Crystal Palace replica.

Hence the present moment:

on a Mitchell Library microfiche
a cub reporter finds
a photo

of a Police Chief looking at
   a photo
   of a nun standing
   on the Giles Gym Coogee Headland
   where she's studying
      the statue
      of Our Lady of the Apparitions
      gazing
           out to sea.

jostle-breezes warm a hesitant bliss
dawn-glossed
on Middle Harbour

sun showers
gum leaf scent
Brubeck muzak moods
misting across the lawn

brickfielder gusts
parch the rose bush
then
coax smoked sighs
from the crackling gum

seeping through tan bark-trash
brackish creek-waters rouse
scorched-dust petrichor

nightfall
soot air cooked in day's last light
salved now by harbour mists pressing

bearing songs that no-one recalls
Kuring-gai smoke
wraps round the Opera House

beach-cave
reflected light scuffs wind-pocked wall
memory blooms in shadowed stench

hunched in fog
gigantic
spine sprung against slate dawn chill:
this Harbour Bridge

no sky   no ground   no figures
swelling bushfire smoke
baulking perspective

a barn
an escarpment
thunder
sheet lightning
two men
twenty greyhounds

paper wasps veering
from spastic reflections
in acrid pondwater

Inner Harbour
oyster beds smudged
with
bushfire cinder dust

weatherboard
the old school-house
a thrown ball
bouncing back
in random jolts

the noise of winter wind at the ear
meanings leaking
where memory stops

quick through The Gap
cold plunging temperature sucks
rainspouts from thunderheads

a chill wind at dusk
undoes the summer
too early
this dread autumn

mottled tumult
in looming cumulus
underlit by western scorch

pock-stoned wind-flutes
flutter-breezes sound-tracking
cove-water scatter-vision

avid gulls bomb
greenwater yaw-swells
sizzling with whitebait sparkle-yen

sandstone stained by tide-shifts
under seeping scarlet
angophora trunks

sunset basting thunderheads —
sudden southerly
slathering waterspouts

cacophonous
vivid squalls of lorikeets
embroidering dawn sky

water tank seeps
man closes barn-door
fruit-bats squeal
black mastiffs slobber

edge-water bubbles pique
in tide-seeps soaked
with slippery sea-grass compost

dry wind at night
printing press on fire
the Aboriginal suburb

midnight switchback intercept
braking wheels howling
breath snatched in descent

sunset slow sighing
heat abating
gulls careening
darkness coming

North Head springtime dawn
billowing thrill
at the salt-tanged ogle station

late-night elation
in automotive speed
taxed quick by happenstance

in tooth-aching pearl-light,
scrape-mouthed dozers gather
on ti-treed green-swale

cupping hands in Harbour water
sensing the size and heft of your heart

cockatoo clamour
angophora blood
sting-ray squads resting at ease

humid dark tunnel-suck
jitter-lit train-express
hurtling through ridge-cuts

lustre in salt spray
spangle in shore break
squabbling harsh scavenger birds

sky quaking seismic
paralysis on ground
scalpel of lightning slash

in the Harbour
a banker afloat
clutching an oversized pumpkin

rain hitting roof then comes hail
cool jazz first
next a rhythm gone Cuban

gouge-water run-off
on slippery ledges
below seeping marsh
frog-stocked

sudden squalls chilling
the stoked daytime heat
sending gusts to peel roofs off

signal box sparking
last train from Lithgow
midnight dream smoke thickening

ache of an old rule
greed-grabbed allotments
no glamour in the gloaming

dawn-sun shadows rousing
ancient whales
engraved on sandstone shelter-ledge

sulphur mist veils
river lurks at bluff body dump
flood that does not flow

pulp slops in harbour nooks
sea fattens up
where
squid flesh clogs
jelly blobs

bubbling blue drink
untouched on a bench —
arrow on floor
painted in blood

rain balm begins
on roasted plains
where
cloudbursts loom in electrical air

moon-steeped glimmers
dawn on sheltered hill-caves
deep with Indigenous time

scatter-pelt hail-stones
mash ibis flocks clamoured
in stabs of spastic light

lullaby bells from treetop birds
anoint
cool green-scented fern-dense groves

rain smelling of sleep
bats squealing in dreams
dome of sky black thundercracked

toffee fragrance glowing out
where rain releases
steaming wattle dust

mantle flicker
thunder shudders shivering glass
buster slamming doors

swelling grove
thronging wattle blossoms glut
toffee sunrise nectar tang

creek seepage tinkles
thunderhead thickens
child yells echoes
down dim dank drain

wattle spangles
under lightning crackle
plovers screech westerly home

night-haul rigs roar
down motorways
ochre-toned
blasted through sandstone bluffs

voltage sky spanning
memory-tracts teaching
seven generations past

gulls flurry thunder-shunted
above warm whorls
of baitfish water

moist blossom spasm
in warm wattle groves
glutting bees
from foreign climes

fog surging tide rise
tugboat thrumming slow
at sluggard super-tanker

guard-rail gone
bright gash across swale
car tumbling into green-water dam

golden dawn dust pollen smatter
parrot drunkards in treetop melee

ocean breeze succumbs to western wind
on ti-tree heath
crisp coastal parch

figure / ground judgement error
soft sun-dazzle
at the diving tower

spanning the Bridge
hot mercy dash
vans + sidecar bikes
in sodium lights

fire hot beyond measure,
taking glade
and
smelting ore from soil

moon burnishing
slack Narabeen lakes
quiet ozone-flush in easeful air

sandstone canyon highway chutes
sending cars to
inner-city boggle maps

stormlight pressing
mists yearn baleful
phosphorescent tides sweep green upswell

rope swinging languid
over pulsing billabong
tiny bubbles popping free

starlight twitters
in southern thunder-glamour
while gales warp lightning strikes

glare stoking sun burn
to roast massed cars
noon-caught
in cross-town thrum muddle

salt wind limns dawnbreak
where high on ridge-lines
gaunt hawks
glide — abide — subside

umber moon looming
from fig-damp miasma
plovers summon storms

weather thickening with firestorm:
aromatic
cinder dust
memory flush

salving lemon-scented gum-tree grove
dark tanging rain tasting of sleep

far west sheet lightning
rain easing down
warm
as
the blood of a chicken

damp sunsetting quiet
where hankering schoolboys
trudge the athletics track

night gulls throng bright tower tops
where
bogong moths swirl
light-drawn
in upswells

distant fire-engine sirens
gliding on night-time
frangipani scent

glossed evening light
sighing cool breath into
lingering daytime heat

bus-drivers
clerks
haberdashers —
the town hosting faces
shaped by their work

thrumming boat waiting
on the wrong side of ripeness
odour emitting

thunderstorm sunset
like
bruises colouring skin
where the knee hinges

launched from that headland to this —
each new squad of birds
fighting rough cross-winds

slow dawn warms eastern roads and bridges
sly birds sing
surfing
first warm updrafts

coarsening moon-wane
when
traceless forces insinuate tide-water swells

strewn across Chinatown —
welts in the shapes
of the actions that made them

freshly parked car
smelling of calamity
clicking while the sun sets

in broiled humid sunlight
new thrusts of wind-change erupt
to blast the air

heat-leaching ebb-strong tidal waters
flotsam clog
bubbling drift-simmer

'eternity'
chalked on courthouse steps —
shy breeze dodging afternoon rain.

bats plummet from hang-trees
to arc on whooshed wings
pumping jabs of dense air

cold Harbour Bridge —
southerly buster veers motorbike
into lane 5

skin-warmth and glare-dazzle change
to chill-squall and thunder
then thumping rain

all fixtures cancelled —
post-twilight gloom lowers
to steepen the grandstand

setting sun warms the west harbour —
safety lights glimmer up cool in the east

now grown heavy with dust —
the hot breeze pressing
from far western deserts

yelping in his pocket
phone-calls to a father
wilting in noon scald

disruption:
    some sly force
    less viscous
    insinuates what's incumbent

wafting ammoniac sludge
     sounds of water struggling
reedy green creek-glut

crown-fire blasts from gum-tree leaf-tops
     blitzing
vast
   budgerigar
         murmurations

sea-breeze ceding to westerly winds
whetting blunt sun
stoking next storm

Kirribilli House:
    limned by coal sun
    backlit with amnesiac fizz

floating
refulgent
jacaranda flakes
adorning the motor-ways

pink sun bastes ash fields
blurred with black flies
clotting mouths of last things breathing

find:
    a brother
    a sister
        their language of grunts
    someone else's tooth

warm rock slab
under foot
the poised shadow of a lone hovering hawk

storm rides in on black bass notes
thrumming all the trees
like harmonic strings

slow ferry
sleek catamaran
each for each
lures its homecoming crowd

warm sleep in dream harbour
bright portents rippling
cold darkness upwelling

chilled wind-shimmer
sudden on estuary-skim —
massed soldier crabs jinking

gum lemon scents
bellbirds
cicadas
moon-looming benediction

this dark pier
breathless unsteady
watching the last homebound ferry
shrink

bright fruits scattered on damp floor
urea tang
cubicle door bolt-locked

magpies dappling
limber lullabies
dawn-trilled to sanctify lulled air

on each heel: a stone bruise;
snubbed in the fob pocket: another man's thumb

ardour abiding —
blushing to remember
what the shy birds were watching

orb-spider web spans path
moths, crickets, bees mangle in the splay,
then you

gentle as wrist-pulse
small fish expiring on ground —
tearful child watching

stuttered footprints stark
in sunrisen mushroom glade —
alibi betrayed

surfer dives board-forward
from rock-ledge to wave-swell —
three strokes till back-surge

asleep near the harbour –
dreams flood a skull
lulled unconscious to canyons

police launch at night
dredging the cold Harbour-shore
with hot panning searchlights

late night ferry fleet:
intricate lanterns adrift
on a vast temple pond

petroleum slick
mutilated sedan
the skewed shape of a scream

damp power lines trembling
rank leaves in wind squabble
quick glandular throbs

spangled spectrum ring
like a church monstrance —
cool moon scoped through ferry spray

dream of a whirlpool
turning to take loved ones
as night folds into day

clap the verso shut
on a slow fat mosquito —
bookmark the future

peppers glimpsed in windblown shrubs
are just the red beaks of vigorous birds

basting glare in homebound train
nodding workers
compressed breath-to-breath

sight-lines down the valleys:
wealth displaying
as if given for taking

a screech from above
stipples on your skin —
bats scatter fig pulp

lightning-flash whip-crack
cove-water
propellor-thrust
bubbles struggling up

window-dazzle
harbour-glitz
ozone air
wooden green ferry traffic

midnight hailstones
aural
aroma-borne
sensory pattern capture

George Street to
Petersham
on Parramatta Road —
that Gadigal track

flushing gold blossom force
cicadas massed in volume
everywhere burgeon

heat haze in the east
plasma blooms above
where the future approaches

skeining ferry smoke
hauling in shy mists
wafting round Taronga wharf

surgewater in winter coves —
quick chime-rhythms struck
on yacht-rigging wires

bubbling black harbour water
holds blunt beasts
unaware sunshine exists

town hall windows all shudder in
sunset so fierce
the thunderstorm growls

aromatic eucalypts
blue-hued
in cascade-glade
moon-anointed

sudden southeaster wind booming
salt spray in ashdrift nectarine dawn

under jetty steps
a bundled thing
softened by blunt repetitions

propellor-torqued throb
sunrise ferry casts off —
one young chaplain on board

black pearl dawn light
on Harbour entrance headlands —
a strengthening toothache

sounds and scents surge
where wattle shrubs circle frog swamp —
ejaculant spring

jitter-lit then pleasure-bit –
new-year's back-street bolt-holers' aftermath

on hard harbour water

vespertine zephyrs chafe

choppy back-smatters of cruiser ships' slops

streets honouring scoundrels —
coins with villains' profiles —
this flash bandit town

hot high-tension lines tremble
in shade-scented gusts
of power-seepage

life-buoys bump and sway
pilot-lights chatter
rain squalls pewter the water

vast
whooshing
vertical
&
vacuum-thrust —
the heat-map of the gone souls

last fumes of daylight
revenant hunger
a man's left ear in the mail

every face a flash card

quick glandular throbs

heartbeat chasing heartbeat

fig-tree in eaves of stock-exchange annexe
money-plant in back-lane skip

swirled liquid silver stars adrift
on black mirror harbour waters
ferry-stirred

tides whelming in moon throb
surge squalls
staggering ferries
clogging car jams

thief's foot caroms
rusty bucket into pitchfork
startling backyard night

children fall from a pedestal
a fist grips a gift
old men sob in a room

swarm locusts borne by western wind
twitching stochastic
on dry park lawns

idle from the train
through damp fig-tree tang —
memories dousing home-town return

voice fuzzed with forgetting
war wounded
no sweetheart
sweeping dirt with a hose

sunset completed
sandstone buildings holding heat
rebuffing night breezes

twinned rainbow at night
dumb luck in a reservoir
commotion on skin

mangroves go quiet
salted message rides the breezes
mud-hoppers snap still

seaside church gilt in dawnlight —
sole statue inside —
ailing, crumbling

south wind blasting sandstone crag —
kids crouch north
in lee-side vacuum-suck

schools of sea-bream
bank sudden solid silver
in rogue green cresting wave

low tide turning quick
jellyfish pumping shorebreak
gulls swooping the rip

electric stabs of light
in motionless air
birds yelling roughneck jeers

rolling
orotund bees
tumbling
clammy
from flurried wattle spangle

touring-circus elephant-stench
thrumming downpour
settling show-ground dust

pained limp of a witness
hamstrung by reminiscence
missed steps in mind

cicada shells on
humming signal box
+
tip-trucks ticking
angle-parked

gleams before dawn
one bird unwinds a scream
agitating the dogs

this perfect mango
too early in springtime —
sick heat in dawn breezes

cold now in the garden
where friends once brought
thoughts to bloom in sunlit talk

sparks flying upward —
one thousand russet locusts
spring from roadside grass

bats tumble from roasted west sky —
thunder buffets
splayed food-franchise-trucks

Did the town grow to these harbour shores?
Or was it uttered from the waters?

frosted dawn light wicks
along deep-water straits
   from fog the town finds form

hazard lights
slow-lane crawl
upturned car
girl stands in fuel-smear
arms upheld

lone drifting cloud
      sun-heat following
  slipstreamed breeze
          forest-tops jostling

memories   flushing   immediate:
creosote tang
weatherboard texture

cold south winds howl in
then gyre up & over
the town's hot concrete core

squalls in bellows surge east through the Heads —
waterspout shrieks up from slate sea

black Harbour night
        no moon   no stars
six red beacon lights   two   six   three   none

Go back to
February 1931.
Let's say Clarice Beckett, the painter,
spent a lost week in Sydney,
adrift on her own in the spangling light.

Imagine
memory is in everything
and
thunder is muttering in the sunsetting west
when
the sky appears plangent, as in a love song,

russet, refulgent,
until it isn't.

Here yesterday
a shy bird was watching
while
children toiled at practising the walk of a chicken —
they were straining for nonchalance,
umbral with shadow friction
and
tottering at a thrilled edge to let otherness in.

Back to nightfall now, in the Middle Harbour, where
sheets of sparkling plankton in wake-water
start pulsating under storm roar.

Shadow-scented, all ozoned,
the ripples on the sandbanks scatter
a fugitive gleam
backstopped with surface tension.

Everywhere, inertia sticks stuttering
under salt sprayed moon lustre
to send a razzle through the shorebreak,
duplicitous — this razzle —

as it limns every separate sight, sound and odour
that marinates the back end of the farthest dark cove.

"There is another world, of course,"
 she says, as if her father is with her,
 as if the sun were still setting,
"but no one expects they'll find it in this one."

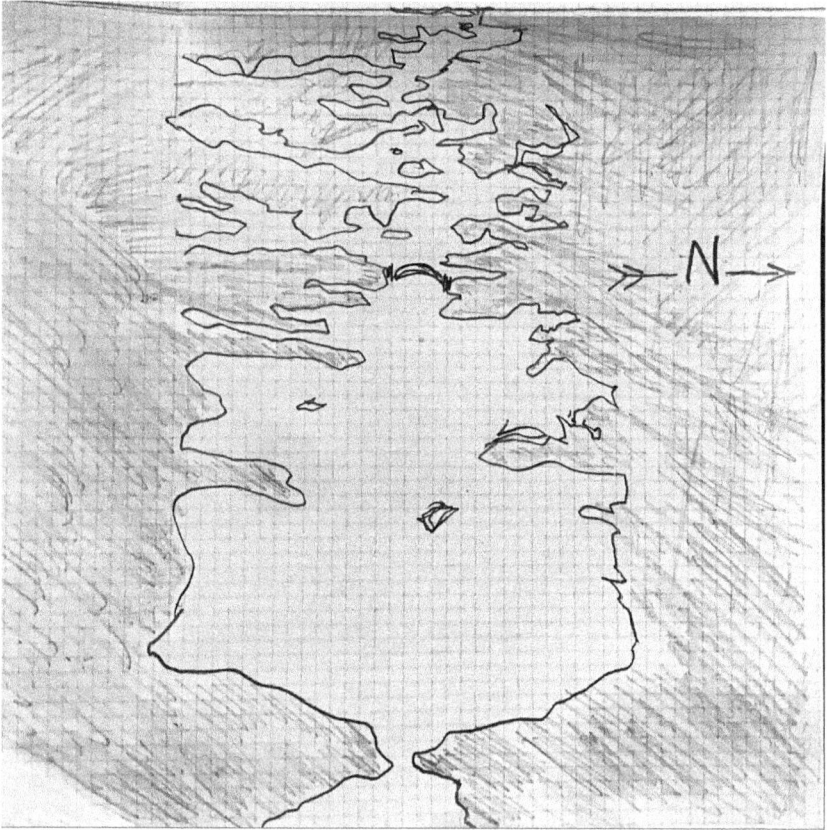

About Upswell

Upswell Publishing was established in 2021 by Terri-ann White as a not-for-profit press. A perceived gap in the market for distinctive literary works in fiction, poetry and narrative non-fiction was the motivation. In her years as a bookseller, writer and then publisher, Terri-ann has maintained a watch on literary books and the way they insinuate themselves into a cultural space and are then located within our literary and cultural inheritance. She is interested in making books to last: books with the potential to still be noticed, and noted, after decades and thus be ripe to influence new literary histories.

About this typeface

Book designer Becky Chilcott chose Foundry Origin not only as a strong, carefully considered, and dependable typeface, but also to honour her late friend and mentor, type designer Freda Sack, who oversaw the project. Designed by Freda's long-standing colleague, Stuart de Rozario, much like Upswell Publishing, Foundry Origin was created out of the desire to say something new.

www.ingramcontent.com/pod-product-compliance
Lightning Source LLC
Chambersburg PA
CBHW030842090426
42737CB00009B/1080